THE MOST BEAUTIFUL PRAYERS OF POPE FRANCIS

Living with Christ

bayard

CONTENTS

"Please, Pray" 5
Prayer to Mary, Mother of the Church and Mother of Our Faith 6
Where Is Your Brother? 8
To the Mother of the Living Gospel 10
A Prayer for Our Earth 14
Through Forgiveness and Mercy 16
Prayer to the Holy Family 20
Joseph, a Model of Holiness 23
Following Pope Francis's Letter to the People of God 24
Prayer for Young People 26
Sunday of the Word of God 28
Mary, Mother of the Amazon 30
Prayer in Times of Epidemic 32
Prayer to the Father of the Human Family 36
Consecration of Russia and Ukraine to the Immaculate Heart of Mary 38
For the Dignity of Indigenous Peoples 40
Prayer for the Marginalized 42
Jubilee of Hope 44
Credits 46

EDITORIAL

On March 13, 2013, when Pope Francis appeared for the first time on the loggia of St. Peter's Basilica, before giving his blessing, he asked everyone to pray for him. This first speech was marked by a new style: simple, direct, and warm.

After welcoming the crowd and speaking to them affectionately, he called for silence, bowed his head, and prayed together with them. This spiritual moment defined what his years of ministry would be like: neither dominating, nor next to the world and the Church, but at its heart, close and fraternal with everyone, carried and uplifted by prayer.

This special edition pays homage to Francis's travels, his texts, and his teachings—all deeply rooted in prayer. In sixteen texts, we rediscover the trajectory of his pontificate and, at his invitation, continue to pray for refugees, the sick, the poor, those wounded by the Church, people at war, families, and our separated brethren.

As Pope Francis models, let us remain present in prayer alongside the peoples of this world, in all circumstances.

FR. SÉBASTIEN ANTONI, A.A.

PRAYER TO MARY, MOTHER OF THE CHURCH AND MOTHER OF OUR FAITH

The first encyclical of Francis, *Lumen fidei* (The Light of Faith), speaks of "the great gift by Jesus." This first text of his pontificate invites us to believe in the future. Strong in his devotion to Mary, the Holy Father suggests to pray to her who, filled with faith, said "yes."

"Mother, help our faith!
Open our ears to hear God's Word
and to recognize his voice and call.
Awaken in us a desire to follow in his footsteps,
to go forth from our own land and to receive his promise.
Help us to be touched by his love,
that we may touch him in faith.
Help us to entrust ourselves fully to him
and to believe in his love, especially at times of trial,
beneath the shadow of the Cross, when our faith is called to mature.
Sow in our faith the joy of the Risen One.
Remind us that those who believe are never alone.
Teach us to see all things with the eyes of Jesus,
that he may be light for our path.
And may this light of faith always increase in us,
until the dawn of that undying day which is Christ himself,
your Son, our Lord! Amen."

"WHERE IS YOUR BROTHER?"

Less than four months after his election, Pope Francis's first trip outside Rome was to Lampedusa, a small Italian island. This visit marked the beginning of a long series of fraternal gestures to migrants and refugees.

The tragic situation of these "brothers and sisters" inspired the Holy Father to offer a prayer of repentance:

"Lord, we beg forgiveness for our indifference to so many of our brothers and sisters.

Father, we ask your pardon for those who are complacent and closed amid comforts which have deadened their hearts; we beg your forgiveness for those who by their decisions on the global level have created situations that lead to these tragedies.

Forgive us, Lord!

Today too, Lord, we hear you asking: 'Adam, where are you?' 'Where is the blood of your brother?' Amen."

TO THE **MOTHER** OF THE **LIVING GOSPEL**

The first apostolic exhortation of Francis, *Evangelii Gaudium* (The Joy of the Gospel), was given at the conclusion of the Year of Faith, opened by Benedict XVI on October 11, 2012. It explains a vision of how to proclaim the Gospel in the heart of the world. This text summarizes the "Francis style."

Inspired by Mary's great faith, the Holy Father proposes this prayer of trust to the Virgin Mary in this exhortation.

"Mary, Virgin and Mother, you who, moved by the Holy Spirit, welcomed the Word of Life in the depths of your humble faith: as you gave yourself completely to the Eternal One, help us to say our own 'yes' to the urgent call, as pressing as ever, to proclaim the Good News of Jesus.

Filled with Christ's presence, you brought joy to John the Baptist, making him exult in the womb of his mother. Brimming over with joy, you sang of the great things done by God. Standing at the foot of the Cross with unyielding faith, you received the joyful comfort of the Resurrection, and joined the disciples in awaiting the Spirit so that the evangelizing Church might be born.

Obtain for us now a new ardor born of the resurrection, that we may bring to all the Gospel of Life which triumphs over death. Give us a holy courage to seek new paths, that the gift of unfading beauty may reach every man and woman.

Virgin of listening and contemplation, Mother of love, Bride of the eternal wedding feast, pray for the Church, whose pure icon you are, that she may never be closed in on herself or lose her passion for establishing God's kingdom.

Star of the new evangelization, help us to bear radiant witness to communion, service, ardent and generous faith, justice and love of the poor, that the joy of the Gospel may reach to the ends of the earth, illuminating even the fringes of our world.

Mother of the living Gospel, wellspring of happiness for God's little ones, pray for us. Amen. Alleluia!"

A PRAYER FOR OUR EARTH

With *Laudato si'* (Praise Be to You), Pope Francis declares a revolutionary encyclical dedicated to ecology. It is part of common efforts between society and the Church to support the urgency of commitment for the respect of nature, noticing that, in the world's "common home," "everything is connected:" ecology, the economy, life together, etc.

Conscious of the urgency, the Holy Father prayed for the "common home" and its inhabitants.

"All powerful God, you are present in the whole universe and in the smallest of your creatures. You embrace with your tenderness all that exists. Pour out upon us the power of your love, that we may protect life and beauty. Fill us with peace, that we may live as brothers and sisters, harming no one.

O God of the poor, help us to rescue the abandoned and forgotten of this earth, so precious in your eyes. Bring healing to our lives, that we may protect the world and not prey on it, that we may sow beauty, not pollution and destruction.

Touch the hearts of those who look only for gain at the expense of the poor and the earth. Teach us to discover the value of each thing, to be filled with awe and contemplation, to recognize that we are profoundly united with every creation as we journey toward your infinite light.

We thank you for being with us each day. Encourage us, we pray, in our struggle for justice, love, and peace. Amen."

THROUGH FORGIVENESS AND MERCY

For the Jubilee of Mercy, from December 8, 2015 to November 20, 2016, Francis invited every believer to perform Corporal Works of Mercy (giving alms, housing the people without lodging, visit those who are sick and in prison, etc.), actions supported by prayer for the Church at the service of the world, in the name of Christ.

Always preferring forgiveness to condemnation, the Holy Father prayed to the Lord of mercy.

"Lord Jesus Christ, you have taught us to be merciful like the heavenly Father, and have told us that whoever sees you sees him. Show us your face and we will be saved. Your loving gaze freed Zacchaeus and Matthew from being enslaved by money; the adulteress and Magdalene from seeking happiness only in created things; made Peter weep after his betrayal, and assured

Paradise to the repentant thief. Let us hear, as if addressed to each one of us, the words that you spoke to the Samaritan woman: 'If you knew the gift of God!'

You are the visible face of the invisible Father, of the God who manifests his power above all by forgiveness and mercy: let the Church be your visible face in the world, its Lord risen and glorified. You willed that your ministers would also be clothed in weakness in order that they may feel compassion for those in ignorance and error: let everyone who approaches them feel sought after, loved, and forgiven by God.

Send your Spirit and consecrate every one of us with its anointing, so that the Jubilee of Mercy may be a year of grace from the Lord, and your Church, with renewed enthusiasm, may bring good news to the poor, proclaim liberty to captives and the oppressed, and restore sight to the blind.

We ask this of you, Lord Jesus, through the intercession of Mary, Mother of Mercy; you who live and reign with the Father and the Holy Spirit for ever and ever. Amen."

PRAYER TO THE HOLY FAMILY

The apostolic exhortation of Francis on love in the family, *Amoris laetitia* (The Joy of Love), was promulgated at the end of a process of reflection for the whole Church, seen to "expose the situation of families in today's world."

The Holy Father, anchored in reality, concludes the text through this prayer.

"Jesus, Mary, and Joseph, in you we contemplate the splendor of true love; to you we turn with trust.

Holy Family of Nazareth, grant that our families too may be places of communion and prayer, authentic schools of the Gospel and small domestic churches.

Holy Family of Nazareth, may families never again experience violence, rejection, and division; may all who have been hurt or scandalized find ready comfort and healing.

Holy Family of Nazareth, make us once more mindful of the sacredness and inviolability of the family, and its beauty in God's plan.
Jesus, Mary, and Joseph, graciously hear our prayer.

Amen."

JOSEPH, A MODEL OF HOLINESS

With the apostolic exhortation *Gaudete et exsultate* (Rejoice and Be Glad), Francis launched a vibrant "call to holiness in today's world." Encouraging joy and hope, he describes five ways to understand the meaning of holiness for today. Page after page, he reminds us that each baptized person has a vocation to joyful holiness.

Here is the prayer that the Holy Father addresses every day to Saint Joseph, protector of the Holy Family.

"Hail, guardian of the Redeemer, spouse of the Blessed Virgin Mary. To you God entrusted his only Son;
in you Mary placed her trust;
with you Christ became man.
Blessed Joseph, to us too, show yourself a father
and guide us in the path of life.
Obtain for us grace, mercy, and courage,
and defend us from every evil. Amen."

FOLLOWING POPE FRANCIS'S LETTER TO THE PEOPLE OF GOD

The Holy Father invites fasting regularly for the victims of pedophilia and for the purification of the Church. This prayer, composed by the bishops of France, was delivered by Bishop Éric de Moulins-Beaufort, President of the Conference of the Bishops of France, during the penitential time in Lourdes on November 6, 2021. It responds to the pope's request for the Universal Church to make an act of repentance and to set a date annually for the victims of sexual violence and aggressions and abuse of power and conscience.

"Forgive us for not having understood how much the power
you give us demands unfailing clarity.
Forgive us for mistaking your mercy for tolerance
in the face of evil. Lift us up, we pray. Remake our hearts.
Inspire us to reach out to those we have
humiliated, neglected, wounded, abandoned.
Lift up the people who suffer, we beg you on our knees.
Let us listen and do what they ask of us.
O God, whom we dare to call "our Father," forgive us.
Remake our hearts. Inspire us to reach out to those
whom we have neglected and abandoned.
Give joy to those we have failed,
we whom you established to carry your word of grace and who have failed.
You have called us to teach, teach us to listen.
You have called us to sanctify, strip us of all appropriation.
May your grace keep us in perpetual conversion.
You have called us to govern, purify us of any taste for power,
free us from all fear, starting with the fear of loss.
God of justice and mercy, God of life and peace,
take pity on us, come to the rescue of our humanity. Amen."

PRAYER FOR YOUNG PEOPLE

In a new kind of synod, the principles of the synodality so dear to Francis are experimented "full scale" with the young people invited to Rome. The apostolic exhortation of the pope *Christus vivit* (Christ Is Alive), promulgated on March 25, 2019 and addressed to "the young and to all the people of God," is the fruit of the synod.

Close to the young and renewed by their enthusiasm, the Holy Father prayed for them during a prayer vigil.

"Lord Jesus, in journeying toward the synod, your Church turns her attention to all the young people of the world. We pray that they might boldly take charge of their lives, aim for the most beautiful and profound things of life, and always keep their hearts unencumbered. Accompanied by wise and generous guides, help them respond to the call you make to each of them, to realize a proper plan of life and achieve happiness.

Keep their hearts open to dreaming great dreams and make them concerned for the good of others. Like the Beloved Disciple, may they stand at the foot of the Cross, to receive your Mother as a gift from you. May they be witnesses to your resurrection and be aware that you are at their side as they joyously proclaim you as Lord. Amen."

SUNDAY OF THE WORD OF GOD

Francis, by his apostolic letter *Aperuit illis* (He Opened Their Intelligence), institutes the Sunday of the Word of God, celebrated each year on the Third Sunday of Ordinary Time. This date sits within the Week of Prayer for Christian Unity and shows the pope's desire to consider the Word to be mediated in relation with our sister Churches.

With the Holy Father, let us pray the Word of God according to the following indications, taken from *Evangelii Gaudium*.

"In the presence of God, during a recollected reading of the text, it is good to ask, for example: 'Lord, what does this text say *to me*? What is it about my life that you want to change by this text? What troubles me about this text? Why am I not interested in this? Or perhaps: What do I find pleasant in this text? What is it about this word that moves me? What attracts me? Why does it attract me?' Amen."

MARY, MOTHER OF THE AMAZON

The apostolic exhortation *Querida Amazonia* (Dear Amazonia) proposes four "dreams" to respond to the "cries" expressed by the people of this region of Latin America. The text interweaves the social, ecological, cultural, and pastoral questions, and aims to be a vigorous defense of the Amazon and its inhabitants.

In conclusion of the exhortation, Francis entrusts Mary to the continent where he was born.

"Mother of life, in your maternal womb Jesus took flesh,
the Lord of all that exists.
Risen, he transfigured you by his light
and made you the Queen of all creation.
For that reason, we ask you, Mary, to reign
in the beating heart of Amazonia...[in] all creatures,

in the beauty of the flowers, the rivers,
the great river that courses through it
and all the life pulsing in its forests.
Tenderly care for this explosion of beauty.
Ask Jesus to pour out all his love
on the men and women who dwell there,
that they may know how to appreciate and care for it.
Bring your Son to birth in their hearts,
so that he can shine forth in the Amazon region,
in its peoples and in its cultures,
by the light of his word,
by his consoling love,
by his message of fraternity and justice.
And at every Eucharist,
may all this awe and wonder be lifted up
to the glory of the Father.
Amen.”

MARCH 11, 2020

PRAYER IN TIMES OF EPIDEMIC

At the height of the first wave of Covid-19, Francis declares that "the Lord wishes to awake and revive our paschal faith." At the heart of a confined Lent, he invited the whole world to join him for a meditation. This time of contemplation is broadcasted to the four corners of the world from a completely empty St. Peter's Square.

Some weeks later, on May 1st, the Holy Father entrusted all those sick from Covid-19 to the Virgin Mary, at the sanctuary of Our Lady of Divine Love, south of Rome.

"O Mary, you always shine on our path
as a sign of salvation and hope.
We entrust ourselves to you, Health of the sick,
at the cross, you united with Jesus' pain keeping steadfast your faith.
You, you know what we need
and we are sure that you will provide
so that, as at Cana of Galilee, joy and celebration
may return after this moment of trial.
Help us, Mother of Divine Love, to conform
to the will of the Father, and to do what we will be told by Jesus,
who took our suffering upon himself
and burdened Himself with our sorrows
to lead us, through the cross,
to the joy of resurrection.

Under your protection we seek refuge, Holy Mother of God.
Do not spurn the pleas of we who are in trial,
and free us from every danger,
O glorious and blessed Virgin. Amen."

PRAYER TO THE FATHER OF THE HUMAN FAMILY

The first words of the encyclical *Fratelli tutti* (All Brothers), like those from *Laudato si'*, are borrowed from Saint Francis of Assisi, whose first name the pope had taken, and concern "rebuilding the Church." For the Holy Father, social friendship and brotherhood are the paths to build a better world, more just and more peaceful, with the commitment of all, people and institutions.

In his close, simple, and warm way, Pope Francis proposed the prayer of brotherhood.

"Lord, Father of our human family,
you created all human beings equal in dignity:
pour forth into our hearts a fraternal spirit
and inspire in us a dream of renewed encounter,
dialogue, justice and peace.
Move us to create healthier societies

and a more dignified world,
a world without hunger, poverty, violence, and war.

May our hearts be open
to all the peoples and nations of the earth.

May we recognize the goodness and beauty
that you have sown in each of us,
and thus forge bonds of unity, common projects,
and shared dreams. Amen."

CONSECRATION OF RUSSIA AND UKRAINE TO THE IMMACULATE HEART OF MARY

During the conflict between Russia and Ukraine, at the end of a penitential celebration in St. Peter's Basilica, Francis renews the consecration of the Church and all humanity to the Immaculate Heart of Mary, in particular the Russian and Ukrainian people.

From the start of the war, the pope renewed the consecration to Mary from Russia, she who, in 1917, had requested it during the apparitions of Fatima (Portugal).

"O Mother, hear our prayer.

Star of the Sea, do not let us be shipwrecked in the tempest of war.

Ark of the New Covenant, inspire projects and paths of reconciliation.

Queen of Heaven, restore God's peace to the world.

Eliminate hatred and the thirst for revenge, and teach us forgiveness.

Free us from war, protect our world from the menace of nuclear weapons.

Queen of the Rosary, make us realize our need to pray and to love.

Queen of the Human Family, show people the path of fraternity.

Queen of Peace, obtain peace for our world. Amen."

JULY 28, 2022

FOR THE DIGNITY OF INDIGENOUS PEOPLES

During his visit to Maskwacis, July 25, 2022, on his trip to Canada, the pope asked forgiveness to the Indigenous people violated by members of the Church. As a sign of rebuilding, he pronounced this prayer addressed to the first bishop of Quebec, François de Laval.

"Let us put into practice these words that we now address to Saint François de Laval," asked the Holy Father.

"You were a man for others, who visited the sick, clothed the poor, defended the dignity of original peoples, supported the strenuous efforts of the missionaries, ever ready to reach out to those worse off than yourself. How many times were your projects frustrated! Each time, however, you took them up again. You understood that God does not build in stone, and that in this land of discouragement, there was a need for a builder of hope."

PRAYER FOR THE MARGINALIZED

On a pastoral visit in France on the occasion of Mediterranean meetings in Marseille and World Day of Migrants and Refugees, the pope proposed in his preparatory message for this day a poignant prayer for exiles.

"God, Father Almighty, grant us the grace to work tirelessly for justice, solidarity, and peace, so that all your children may enjoy the freedom to choose whether to migrate or to stay.

Grant us the courage to denounce the all horrors of our world, and to combat every injustice that mars the beauty of your children and the harmony of our common home.

Sustain us by the power of your Spirit, so that we can reflect your tender love to every migrant you place in our path, and to spread in hearts and in every situation the culture of encounter and of care. Amen."

JUBILEE OF HOPE

On December 24, 2024, Francis inaugurated the Holy Year, dedicated to hope. In his speech, he reminded us that God always forgives and invites everyone to welcome this grace. This jubilee calls us to meet the Lord and to bring hope where it is lacking: with the poor, prisoners, victims of the war, and all the wounded lives. A true reflection of the main lines of his pontificate.

"Father in heaven, may the *faith* you have given us in your son, Jesus Christ, our brother, and the flame of *charity* enkindled in our hearts by the Holy Spirit, reawaken in us the blessed *hope* for the coming of your Kingdom.

May your grace transform us into tireless cultivators of the seeds of the Gospel. May those seeds transform from within both humanity and the whole cosmos in the sure expectation of a new heaven and a new earth, when, with the powers of Evil vanquished, your glory will shine eternally.

May the grace of the Jubilee reawaken in us, *Pilgrims of Hope*, a yearning for the treasures of heaven. May that same grace spread the joy and peace of our Redeemer throughout the earth. To you our God, eternally blessed, be glory and praise for ever. Amen."

HINC VBERES SCATEANT DIVINAE GRA
TIAE LATICES OMNIVMQVE INGREDIEN
TIVM ANIMOS EXPIENT ALMA REFI
CIANT PACE CHRISTIANA VIRTVTE
EXORNENT ANNO SACRO MCML

Special Issue
Living with Christ

PUBLISHER: David Dziena
ASSOCIATE PUBLISHER: Father John Franck, A.A.
EDITOR: Terence Hegarty
PROJECT EDITOR: Rita Advent
DESIGN: Jeff McCall

Sponsored by the Augustinians of the Assumption
PROVINCIAL: Father Chi Ai Nguyen, A.A.

Bayard, Inc.
500 Salisbury St. ■ Worcester, MA 01609
PHONE: (800) 214-3386
WEBSITE: www.livingwithchrist.us
EMAIL: LWC@bayardfaithresources.com

ISBN: 978-1-62785-856-4
Printed in the U.S.A.

bayard

FSC
MIX
Paper | Supporting responsible forestry
FSC® C021872

Photo Credits

COVER & PAGE 4: Eric Vandeville/ABACA

PAGE 6: PATRICIA DE MELO MOREIRA/AFP via Getty Images

PAGE 9: Gregorio Borgia/AP/SIPA

PAGE 10: Franco Origlia/Getty Images

PAGE 12: Alessia Giuliani/Vatican Pool - Corbis/Corbis via Getty Images

PAGE 14: stock.adobe.com/1xpert

PAGE 18: © Vatican Media via Vatican Pool/Getty Images

PAGE 19: © Mondadori Portfolio via Getty Images

PAGE 21: Franco Origlia/Getty Images

PAGE 22: © Vatican Media/Abacapress.com

PAGE 26: Committee for the 2014 Papal Visit to Korea via Getty Images

PAGE 29: © Vincenzo Pinto/AFP

PAGE 31: stock.adobe.com/akepong srichaichana

PAGE 32: Vatican Pool - Corbis/Getty Images

PAGE 34-35: © Maurix/Gamma Rapho

PAGE 37: Franco Origlia/Getty Images

PAGE 41: © PATRICK T. FALLON/AFP via Getty Images

PAGE 43: Vatican Media via Vatican Pool/Getty Images

PAGE 45: ALBERTO PIZZOLI/POOL/AFP via Getty Images